ON THIS DAT

A Unique Glimpse at What ELSE Happened on YOUR Day!

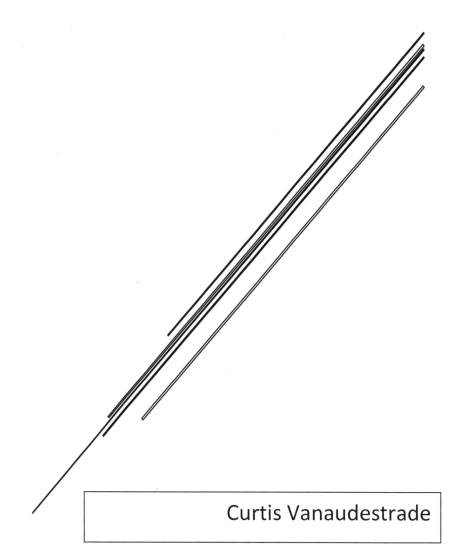

Curtis Vanaudestrade

©2017 Curtis Vanaudestrade
All Rights Reserved

"Study the past if you would define the future."
— **Confucius**

April 14

Year	Event
43 BC	Mark Antony went after Caesar's assassin, Brutus, in Mutina but was then beaten by Hirtius
69	Vitellius, commander of the Rhine armies, defeated Emperor Otho in the Battle of Bedriacum and seized the throne
70	Titus, son of Roman Emperor Vespasian, surrounded Jerusalem with four Roman legions
193	Septimius Severus was proclaimed Roman Emperor by the army in Illyricum (in the Balkans)
754	Pact of Quierzy, in which the Franks were obliged to defend papal interests between Pope Stephen II, and Pippin the Korte
911	Sergius III, the 119th Pope, died
966	Polish pagan ruler Mieszko I converted to Christianity, this was regarded as the founding of the Polish state
972	Notger became bishop of Liege, Belgium
979	Challenge to throne of King Aethelred II of England
1028	Henry III became King of the Germans
1132	Mstislav I Grand Prince of Kiev died at age 55
1191	Henry VI was crowned in Rome, Italy as Emperor of the Holy Roman Empire by Pope Colestine III

Year	Event
1205	The Bulgarians and the Crusaders clashed in the Battle of Adrianople in Bulgaria
1294	Temür, grandson of Kublai, was elected Khagan of the Mongols and Emperor of the Yuan Dynasty with the reigning titles Oljeitu and Chengzong
1341	Sack of Saluzzo, Italy by Italian-Angevine troops under Manfred V of Saluzzo occurred
1434	The foundation stone of Cathedral St. Peter and St. Paul in Nantes, France was laid
1471	The Yorkists under Edward IV defeated the Lancastrians under the Earl of Warwick at the Battle of Barnet; the Earl is killed and Edward IV resumed the English throne
1536	English King Henry VIII expropriated minor monasteries
1543	The 2nd in command to Juan Rodriguez Cabrillo returned the exploration fleet back to Berra de Navidad, Mexico after the death of Cabrillo
1544	Battle at Carignano: French troops under Earl d'Enghien beat Swiss
1570	Polish Calvinists/Lutherans/Hernhutters unify against Jesuits
1574	Battle of Mookerhei - D'Avila beat Louis of Nassau
1578	Future King of Portugal and Spain, Philip II, was born

1611 The word "telescope" was first used by Prince Federico Cesi, Italian scientist, naturalist, and founder of the Accademia dei Lincei. He and Galileo were contemporaries and supported one another's work.

1629 England and France signed the Peace of Susa

1639 Saxony Imperial forces were defeated by the Swedes at the Battle of Chemnitz

1671 Cossacks captured Russian peasant leader Stenka Razin

1699 Birth of Khalsa, the brotherhood of the Sikh religion, in Northern India according to the Nanakshahi calendar

1715 The Yamasee War began in South Carolina between the early settlers and the natives

1738 Future British Prime Minister Cavendish-Bennick was born

1741 Emperor Momozono of Japan was born

1756 Governor Glen of South Carolina protests against 900 Acadia Indians

1759 Composer George Frederick Handel died in London

1773 Jean-Baptiste de Villèle, French politician, 6th Prime Minister of France was born

1775 Benjamin Franklin and Benjamin Rush organized the first American society for the abolition of slavery

1777 New York adopted a new constitution as an independent state

1792 France declared war on Austria, starting the French Revolutionary War

1793 A royalist rebellion in Santo Domingo was crushed by French republican troops

1812 Future New Zealand Premier George Grey was born in Lisbon, Portugal

1818 US Medical Corps formed

1828 Noah Webster published his first edition of *American Dictionary of the English Language*

1828 British 18-gun sloop *HMS Acorn* sank off Halifax with 115 men aboard

1831 Soldiers marching on a bridge in Manchester, England, caused it to collapse

1836 US Congress formed Territory of Wisconsin

1841 Edgar Allan Poe published the first detective story, "*Murders in the Rue Morgue*"

1846 The Donner Party of pioneers departed Springfield, Illinois, for California, on what would become a year-long journey of hardship, cannibalism, and survival in the Sierra Nevada Mountains

1847 Persia and Ottoman Turkey signed the 2nd Treaty of Erzurum

1849 Hungary declared its' independence from Austria

1860 The first Pony Express rider reached San Francisco, California, having ridden all the way from St. Joseph, Missouri

1861 The formal Union surrender of Ft Sumter in the US Civil War took place

1863 William Bullock patented continuous-roll printing press

1864 The Battle of Fort Pillow, Tennessee took place, resulting in the deaths of over 300 African-American Union soldiers. Although the soldiers had surrendered, and should have been taken as prisoners of war, the Confederates chose to kill them instead. From then on the Union refused to engage in prisoner exchanges.

1865 U.S. President Lincoln was shot at Ford's Theatre in Washington, DC and died hours later. At the same time, Secretary of State John Seward and his family were attacked in their Washington, DC home

1865 Mobile, Alabama was captured by Union forces in the US Civil War

1868 South Carolina voters approved their new state constitution, 70,758 to 27,228

1871 Canada set denominations of currency as dollars, cents, and mills

1872 Dominion Lands Act passed, which is Canada's Homestead Act

1872 San Francisco organized its' Bar Association

1881 The notorious gunfight *Four Dead in Five Seconds* occurred in El Paso, Texas

1883 Leo Delibes' opera "*Lakmé*" premiered in Paris

1887 Start of Sherlock Holmes adventure "*Reigate Squires*"

1894 The first ever public motion picture house opened in New York City, with the first public showing of Thomas Edison's kinetoscope moving pictures

1895 The first performance of Gustav Mahler's (incomplete) *2nd Symphony* took place

1900 Veteran's Hospital at Ft Miley was formed

1902 James C Penney opened his first store, in Kammerer, Wyoming, calling it *"The Golden Rule"*

1903 Dr Harry Plotz discovered a vaccine against typhoid in New York City

1904 George Bernard Shaw's "*Candida*" premiered in London

1906 US President Theodore Roosevelt denounced "muckrakers" in US press, taken from John Bunyan's Pilgrim's Progress

1907 François Duvalier, Haitian politician, 40th President of Haiti was born

1909 Anglo-Persian Oil Company formed in London

1910 U.S. President William Howard Taft threw out the first ball for the Washington Senators and the Philadelphia Athletics

1911 Henri Elzéar Taschereau, Canadian jurist, 4th Chief Justice of Canada, died at age 74

1912 *The Titanic* collided with an iceberg and began sinking. The Marconi room of the ship used the Morse code SOS for the first time ever

1912 Fenway Park opened in Boston

1912 Henri Brisson, French politician, 50th Prime Minister of France died at age 76

1913 Belgium began a general strike for voting rights

1914 Stacy G Carkhuff patented non-skid tire pattern

1915 Dutch merchant navy ship *Katwijk* was sunk by a German torpedo

1915 Turkey invaded Armenia

1918 Pilots of the US First Aero Squadron had their first dogfight over the western front during World War I, shooting down two German planes

1919 Following Gandhi's nonviolent methods, Muslim and Hindu protested British rule; British troops fire on the crowds, killing 400

1920 In Tampa, Florida 6,400 workers in 27 cigar factories walked off beginning a 10-month strike

1921 In the NHL Championship the Ottawa Senators swept the Toronto St Patricks in 2 games

1921 Prince Henry opened Rotterdam-Amsterdam-Bremen-Hamburg air route

1922 Audrey Long, American actress was born

1922 Jeanette Vreeland sang the first radio concert from an airplane as she flew over New York City

1922 Republic rebels occupied 4 government courts in Dublin

1923 Roberto De Vicenzo, Argentinian golfer was born

1924 Shorty Rogers, American trumpet player and composer was born

1924 Joseph Ruskin, American actor was born

1924 Philip Stone, English actor was born

1925 Abel Muzorewa, Zimbabwean politician, 1st Prime Minister of Zimbabwe Rhodesia was born

1925 Rod Steiger, American actor was born

1925 WGN became the first radio station to broadcast a regular season major league baseball game. The Cubs beat the Pirates 8-2.

1926 Barbara Anderson, New Zealand author was born

1926 Liz Renay, American actress and author was born

1927 The first *Volvo* auto premiered in Gothenburg, Sweden

1927 Dany Robin, French actress was born

1928 The Bremen, a German Junkers W33 type aircraft, reached Greenly Island, Canada, the first successful transatlantic aeroplane flight from east to west

1928 *Maddus Airlines* began the first regular passenger flights between San Francisco and Los Angeles

1928 In the Stanley Cup the NY Rangers beat the Montreal Maroons, 3 games to 2

1929 The Grand Prix of Monaco was born

1929 Inez Andrews, American singer-songwriter (The Caravans) was born

1930 Bradford Dillman, American actor and author was born

1930 Jay Robinson, American actor was born

1930 Philip Barry's "*Hotel Universe*" premiered in NYC

1931 Spain's King Alfonso XIII went into exile and the Spanish revolution was proclaimed

1931 The first edition of *the Highway Code* was published in Great Britain

1931 In the Stanley Cup the Montreal Canadiens beat the Chicago Blackhawks, 3 games to 2

1932 Atef Ebeid, Egyptian academic and politician, 47th Prime Minister of Egypt was born

1932 Bizet, Massine and Mira's "*Jeux d'Enfants*" premiered in Monte Carlo

1932 Bob Grant, English actor was born

1932 Loretta Lynn, American singer-songwriter and guitarist was born

1933 Shani Wallis, British-American actress was born

1935 "Black Sunday Storm", the worst dust storm of the U.S. Dust Bowl struck

1936 Arlene Martel, American actress and singer was born

1936 Bobby Nichols, American golfer was born

1939 John Steinbeck's novel *The Grapes of Wrath* was published

1940 Julie Christie, Anglo-Indian actress was born

1940 Allied troops landed in Norway

1940 RCA demonstrated its new electron microscope in Philadelphia

1941 Nazi German General Erwin Rommel attacked Tobruk during World War II

1941 Julie Christie, Indian-English actress was born

1941 Pete Rose, American baseball player and manager was born

1941 The first massive German raid in Paris, 3,600 Jews rounded up

1941 King Peter left Yugoslavia

1942 Destroyer *Roper* sank German *U-85* off the US east coast

1943 Fouad Siniora, Lebanese politician, 65th Prime Minister of Lebanon was born

1943 During World War II, Generals Alexander, Eisenhower, Anderson and Bradley met to discuss an assault on Tunis

1943 James Gow and A d'Usseau's "*Tomorrow the World*" premiered in New York City

1943 A JN-25 decrypt by American intelligence detailing a forthcoming visit by Marshal Admiral Yamamoto to Balalae Island results in his plane shot down 4 days later

1944 A massive explosion in Bombay harbor India killed 300 and caused economic damage valued then at 20 million pounds

1944 John Sergeant, English journalist was born

1944 The first Jews transported from Athens arrived at Auschwitz

1944 General Eisenhower became the Supreme Allied Commander of the Allied Expeditionary Force

1944 Greek Colonel Venizelos formed a government

1945 Osijek, Croatia was liberated from Italian Fascist occupation

1945 Tuilaepa Aiono Sailele Malielegaoi, Samoan politician, 8th Prime Minister of Samoa was born

1945 Ritchie Blackmore, English guitarist and songwriter (*The Outlaws, Deep Purple, Rainbow, and Blackmore's Night*) was born

1945 Roger Frappier, Canadian actor, director, producer, and screenwriter was born

1945 American planes bombed Tokyo and damaged the Imperial Palace

1945 Arnhem and Zwolle were freed from Nazis by Allied forces

1945 The US 7th Army and Allied forces captured Nuremberg and Stuttgart in Germany

1945 US forces conquered Motobu peninsula on Okinawa

1945 US Marines attacked Yae Take on Okinawa

1946 The civil war between Communists and Nationalists resumed in China.

1946 Mireille Guiliano, French-American author was born

1946 Knut Kristiansen, Norwegian pianist and orchestra leader was born

1946 "*Day Before Spring*" closed at National Theater in New York City

1947 Dominique Baudis, French journalist and politician was born

1948 Berry Berenson, American model, actress, and photographer was born

1948 A flash of light was observed in crater Plato on Moon

1948 New York City subway fares jumped from 5 cents to 10 cents

1948 In the Stanley Cup the Toronto Maple Leafs swept the Detroit Red Wings in 4 games

1949 Chris Langham, English actor and screenwriter was born

1949 John Shea, American actor and director was born

1949 Dave Gibbons, English author and illustrator was born

- **1949** International Military Tribunal at Nuremberg issued its last judgment
- **1950** Péter Esterházy, Hungarian author was born
- **1950** The first edition of British comic "*Eagle*" was published
- **1950** Doorne's Auto factory opened in the Netherlands
- **1951** Al Christie, Canadian-American director, producer, and screenwriter died at age 69
- **1951** Julian Lloyd Webber, English cellist, conductor, and educator was born
- **1951** Elizabeth Symons, Baroness Symons of Vernham Dean, English politician was born
- **1953** Viet Minh invaded Laos with 40,00 troops
- **1953** WHYN (now WGGB) TV channel 40 in Springfield-Holyoke, MA (ABC) began broadcasting
- **1954** Bruce Sterling, American author was born
- **1954** Katsuhiro Otomo, Japanese director, screenwriter, and illustrator was born
- **1954** Soviet diplomat Vladimir Petrov asked for political asylum in Canberra
- **1955** Fats Domino's *Ain't That a Shame* was released
- **1955** In the Stanley Cup the Detroit Red Wings beat the Montreal Canadiens, 4 games to 3, 2nd year in a row
- **1955** WBRZ TV channel 2 in Baton Rouge, LA (ABC/NBC) began broadcasting

1956 The Anpex Corp first demonstrated the video tape recorder in Chicago, Illinois

1956 Boris Šprem, Croatian politician, 8th President of Croatian Parliament was born

1956 Barbara Bonney, American soprano was born

1956 "*Plain and Fancy*" closed at Mark Hellinger Theater in New York City after 476 performances

1957 Lothaire Bluteau, Canadian actor was born

1957 Mikhail Pletnev, Russian pianist, composer, and conductor was born

1957 Richard Jeni, American comedian and actor was born

1958 The Soviet satellite Sputnik 2 fell from orbit after a 162-day mission and burned up in the atmosphere with passenger dog Laika

1958 Peter Capaldi, Scottish actor, director, and screenwriter was born

1958 John D'Aquino, American actor was born

1958 Van Cliburn won the International Tchaikovsky piano competition and appeared on national TV for the first time. He was on NBC's *The Tonight Show* with Jack Paar

1959 The Taft Memorial Bell Tower was dedicated in Washington, DC.

1959 KDIN TV channel 11 in Des Moines, IA (PBS) began broadcasting

1960 Brian Forster, American actor was born

1960 Brad Garrett, American comedian and actor was born

1960 Tina Rosenberg, American journalist and author was born

1960 The musical *Bye Bye Birdie* opened in New York City

1960 The first underwater launching of a Polaris missile took place

1960 Myoma Myint Kywe, Burmese historian and journalist was born

1960 Osamu Sato, Japanese graphic artist, programmer, and composer was born

1960 In the Stanley Cup the Montreal Canadiens swept the Toronto Maple Leafs in 4 games

1961 The Bay of Pigs invasion took place in Cuba in an attempt to overthrow Castro but failed

1961 Robert Carlyle, Scottish actor was born

1961 Daniel Clowes, American cartoonist and screenwriter was born

1961 The first live television broadcast from Soviet Union took place

1961 US element 103 (Lawrencium) was discovered

1962 Demonstration for sovereign status of New-Guinea took place in Amsterdam

1962 Georges Pompidou became Prime Minister of France after the resignation of Michel Debré

1963 *The Beatles* met *The Rolling Stones* after a Stones concert in Richmond, England.

1964 Gina McKee, English actress was born

1964 Jeff Andretti, American race car driver was born

1964 Greg Battle, American-Canadian football player was born

1965 Kirk Windstein, English-American singer-songwriter and guitarist (*Crowbar, Down, Valume Nob, and Kingdom of Sorrow*) was born

1965 Millie Small appeared on ABC-TV's *Shindig!* and performed her song *My Boy Lollipop*

1965 Tom Dey, American director and producer was born

1965 Alexandre Jardin, French author was born

1966 David Justice, American baseball player and sportscaster was born

1966 Greg Maddux, American baseball player, coach, and manager was born

1967 Gnassingbé Eyadéma overthrew President of Togo Nicolas Grunitzky and installed himself as the new president

1967 Barrett Martin, American drummer, producer, and songwriter (*Mad Season, Screaming Trees, Skin Yard, and Tuatara*) was born

1967 Julia Zemiro, French-Australian actress and singer was born

1967 The *Bee Gees* released their first English single. It was *New York Mining Disaster 1941*

1967 The final *Where the Action Is* aired on ABC-TV

1967 In the Vietnam War, US planes bombed Haiphong for the first time

1967 Steve Chiasson, Canadian ice hockey player was born

1967 Alain Côté, Canadian ice hockey player was born

1968 Roberto de Vicenzo lost the Masters golf tournament for signing an incorrect score card

1968 2 Americans were killed in the DMZ (de-militarized zone) between North and South Korea by a North Korean infiltration team

1968 Anthony Michael Hall, American actor, director, and producer was born

1969 For the first time, a major league baseball game was played in Montreal, Canada.

1969 Martyn LeNoble, Dutch-American bass player (*Porno for Pyros*, *Jane's Addiction, and Thelonious Monster*) was born

1969 The *33 1/3 Revolutions Per Monkee* TV special aired on NBC

1969 Brad Ausmus, American baseball player and manager was born

1969 Vebjørn Selbekk, Norwegian journalist was born

1969 KEET TV channel 13 in Eureka, CA (PBS) began broadcasting

1969 The Student Afro-American Society (SAS) seized the Columbia College admissions office and demanded a special admissions board and staff

1969 A tornado struck Dacca, East Pakistan killing 540

1970 Shizuka Kudō, Japanese singer and actress (*Onyanko Club*) was born

1970 Stephen Stills broke his wrist in an auto accident

1970 Emre Altuğ, Turkish singer-songwriter and actor was born

1970 Steve Avery, American baseball player was born

1970 "*Boy Friend*" opened at Ambassador Theater in New York City for 119 performances

1971 Carlos Pérez, Dominican-American baseball player was born

1971 Gregg Zaun, American baseball player and sportscaster was born

1971 Fort Point, San Francisco was dedicated as a national historic site

1971 President Nixon ended the blockade against the People's Republic of China

1971 Stephen Sondheim's musical "*Follies*" premiered in New York City

1971 The US Supreme Court upheld busing as means of achieving racial desegregation

1972 Roberto Mejía, Dominican baseball player was born

1972 Dean Potter, American rock climber and BASE jumper was born

1972 The Provisional Irish Republican Army exploded twenty-four bombs in towns and cities across Northern Ireland

1973 Adrien Brody, American actor and producer was born

1973 David Miller, American tenor and actor (*Il Divo*) was born

1973 Acting FBI director L Patrick Gray resigned after admitting he destroyed evidence in the Watergate scandal

1974 Da Brat, American rapper and actress was born

1975 Lita, American wrestler and singer (*The Luchagors*) was born

1975 Fredric March, American actor died at age 77

1975 Avner Dorman, Israeli-American composer and academic was born

1976 Christian Älvestam, Swedish singer-songwriter and guitarist (*Scar Symmetry, Miseration, and Solution .45*) was born

1976 Motown Records and Stevie Wonder held a news conference to announce he had signed a "$13 million-plus" contract with the label

1976 *Bay City Roller* singer Eric Faulkner almost died after swallowing Seconal and Valium tablets

1976 Georgina Chapman, English model, actress, and fashion designer, co-founder of Marchesa was born

1976 Anna DeForge, American basketball player was born

1976 Kyle Farnsworth, American baseball player was born

1976 Jason Wiemer, Canadian ice hockey player was born

1977 Sarah Michelle Gellar, American actress and producer was born

1977 Nate Fox, American basketball player was born

1977 Rob McElhenney, American actor, producer, and screenwriter was born

1977 JD McPherson, American singer-songwriter was born

1977 Sarah Michelle Gellar, American actress and producer was born

1977 US Supreme Court ruled that people may refuse to display state motto on their car license plate

1978 Thousands of Georgians demonstrated against Soviet attempts to change the constitutional status of the Georgian language

1978 Paul O'Brien, South African-Australian actor was born

1978 Joe Gordon, American baseball player and manager died at age 62

1978 David Hare's "*Plenty*" premiered in London

1978 A Korean Air Lines Boeing 707, was fired on by Soviets, and crashed in Russia

1978 WRR-AM in Dallas Texas changed call letters to KAAM

1979 Patrick Somerville, American novelist and short story writer was born

1979 Rebecca DiPietro, American wrestler and model was born

1979 Kerem Tunçeri, Turkish basketball player was born

1980 Win Butler, American-Canadian singer-songwriter and guitarist (*Arcade Fire*) was born

1980 Claire Coffee, American actress was born

1980 A New Jersey state assemblyman introduced a resolution to make Bruce Springsteen's *Born to Run* the official state song.

1980 *Iron Maiden's* self-titled debut album was released.

1980 Gary Numan released "*The Touring Principle*," a 45-minute concert video. It was the first commercially available home rock videocassette

1980 The first Cubans of the Mariel boatlift sail to Florida

1981 The first space shuttle flight successfully ended when the *Columbia* landed at Edwards Air Force base in California

1981 Amy Leach, English director and producer was born

1983 Pete Farndon (*Pretenders*) died of a drug overdose at the age of 29. He had been fired from the band the year before due to his drug problem

1983 William Obeng, Ghanaian-American football player was born

1983 Nikoloz Tskitishvili, Georgian basketball player was born

1983 US President Reagan signed a $165 billion Social Security rescue

1984 The Texas Board of Education began requiring that the state's public school textbooks describe the evolution of human beings as "theory rather than fact".

1984 Adán Sánchez, American singer-songwriter was born

1984 Blake Costanzo, American football player was born

1984 Tyler Thigpen, American football player was born

1985 Noele Gordon, English actress died at age 65

1985 The Russian paper "*Pravda*" called U.S. President Reagan's planned visit to Bitburg to visit the Nazi cemetery an "act of blasphemy"

1985 Grant Clitsome, Canadian ice hockey player was born

1985 Alan Garcia won elections in Peru

1986 In retaliation for the April 5 bombing in West Berlin that killed two U.S. servicemen, U.S. President Reagan ordered major bombing raids against Libya, killing 60

1986 Author Simone de Beauvoir died in Paris at age 78

1986	Double-decker ferry sank in stormy weather in Bangladesh killing 200
1987	Soviet leader Mikhail Gorbachev proposed banning all missiles from Europe
1987	Turkey asked to join European market
1988	The USS *Samuel B. Roberts* struck a mine in the Persian Gulf during Operation Earnest Will.
1988	The Soviet Union signed an agreement in Geneva, Switzerland pledging to withdraw its troops from Afghanistan
1988	In New York, real estate tycoons Harry and Leona Helmsley were indicted for income tax evasion
1988	Brad Sinopoli, Canadian football player was born
1989	Tom Petty released his first solo album *Full Moon Fever*
1989	Joe Haden, American football player was born
1989	The $1,100,000,000^{th}$ Chinese baby was born
1989	In the Iran-Contra trial, Oliver North's case went to the jury
1990	Thurston Harris, American singer died at age 58
1990	Cal Ripken of the Baltimore Orioles began a streak of 95 errorless games and 431 total chances by a shortstop.
1991	The Republic of Georgia declared its' independence from the Soviet Union

1991 "*Mule Bone*" closed at Ethel Barrymore Theater in New York City after 67 performances

1991 "*Oh, Kay!*" closed at Lunt-Fontanne Theater in New York City

1992 "*Guys and Dolls*" opened at Martin Beck Theater in New York City for 1,143 performances

1992 "*Les Miserables*" opened at Palace Theatre, Manchester

1992 A court threw out *Apple*'s lawsuit against *Microsoft*

1992 UAW (United Auto Workers' Union) ended a 5-month strike against Caterpillar Inc.

1992 A UN imposed embargo against Libya took effect

1993 In South Africa, millions of black workers went on strike to protest the slaying of activist Chris Hani

1993 Vivien Cardone, American actress, was born

1993 Graham Phillips, American actor and singer, was born

1993 Burnell Taylor, American singer was born

1993 Ellington Ratliff, American drummer was born

1994 In a U.S. friendly fire incident during Operation Provide Comfort in northern Iraq, two United States Air Force aircraft mistakenly shot down two United States Army helicopters, killing 26

1994 Skyler Samuels, American actress was born

1994 Jacqueline Kennedy Onassis was operated on for a bleeding ulcer

1995 Burl Ives, American actor and singer, died at age 85

1996 Abigail Breslin, American actress was born

1998 Virginia executed Paraguayan Francisco Berard who has been convicted of murder

1999 NATO mistakenly bombed a convoy of ethnic Albanian refugees – Yugoslav officials say 75 were killed

1999 A severe hailstorm strikes Sydney, Australia causing $2.3 billion in insured damages, the costliest natural disaster in Australian history

1999 Ellen Corby, American actress died at age 87

1999 Anthony Newley, English-American singer-songwriter and actor died at age 67

1999 Pakistan test-fired a ballistic missile that was capable of carrying a nuclear warhead and reaching its rival neighbor India

1999 Bill Wendell, American television announcer died at age 74

1999 Tammy Wynette's body was exhumed and an autopsy performed in Nashville at the request of her husband, George Richey.

1999 It was reported that Prince intended to re-record the entire catalog of his music and re-release it.

2000 Protesters in Washington, DC dumped manure on Pennsylvania Avenue in an attempt to disrupt meetings of the World Bank and the International Monetary Fund

2000 After five years of deadlock, Russia approved the START II treaty that calls for the scrapping of U.S. and Russian nuclear warheads. The Russian government warned it would abandon all arms-control pacts if Washington continued with an anti-missile system

2001 Hiroshi Teshigahara, Japanese director, producer, and screenwriter died at age 73

2002 Venezuelan President Hugo Chávez returned to office two days after being ousted and arrested by the country's military

2002 U.S. President George W. Bush sent a letter of congratulations to JC Penny's associates for being in business for 100 years. James Cash (J.C.) Penney had opened his first retail store on April 14, 1902.

2003 U.S. troops in Baghdad captured Abu Abbas, leader of the Palestinian group that killed an American on the hijacked cruise liner the MS *Achille Lauro* in 1985

2003 The Human Genome Project was completed with 99% of the human genome sequenced to an accuracy of 99.99%

2004 Micheline Charest, English-Canadian television producer, co-founder of the *Cookie Jar Group* died at age 50

2005 The Oregon Supreme Court nullified marriage licenses issued to gay couples a year earlier by Multnomah County

2005 John Fred, American singer-songwriter died at age 63

2006 Ariel Charon ended his term as the Prime Minister of Israel and Ehud Olmert became the Prime Minister

2007 Entertainer Don Ho, who became the voice of Hawaii, died in Waikiki at the age of 76

2007 At least 200,000 demonstrators in Ankara, Turkey protested against the possible candidacy of incumbent Prime Minister Recep Tayyip Erdoğan

2007 June Callwood, Canadian journalist, author, and activist died at age 82

2008 *Delta Air Lines* and *Northwest Airlines* announced they were combining

2008 Tommy Holmes, American baseball player and manager, died at age 90

2008 Ollie Johnston, American animator and voice actor, died at age 95

2009 Maurice Druon, French author, died at age 90

2010 Nearly 2,700 were killed in a 6.9 earthquake in Yushu, Qinghai, China

2010 Peter Steele, American singer-songwriter and bass player (*Type O Negative, Carnivore, and Fallout*), died at age 47

2010 Icelandic Volcano Eyjafjallajökull began erupting from the top crater in the center of the glacier

2012 Jonathan Frid, Canadian actor died at age 87

2012 William Finley, American actor died at age 71

2012 Émile Bouchard, Canadian ice hockey player and coach died at age 92

2012 Martin Poll, American film producer died at age 89

2013 George Jackson, American singer-songwriter died at age 67

2013 Armando Villanueva, Peruvian politician, 121st Prime Minister of Peru died at age 97

2013 Colin Davis, English conductor and educator died at age 85

2013 Rentarō Mikuni, Japanese actor and director died at age 89

2013 20 were killed in attacks in Mogadishu, Somalia

2013 33 were killed after a bus tumbled off a cliff in Trujillo, Peru

2013 11 were killed and 50 are injured after a hotel fire in Xiangyang, China

2013 Justin Trudeau, son of long-serving Canadian Prime Minister Pierre Trudeau, was elected leader of the Liberal Party of Canada

2014 Twin bomb blasts in Abuja, Nigeria, killed at least 75 and injured 141 others

2014 Crad Kilodney, Canadian author died at age 65

2014 276 schoolgirls were abducted by Boko Haram in Chibok, Northeastern Nigeria, sparking global outrage and the viral #BringBackOurGirls social media campaign

2014 Armando Peraza, Cuban-American drummer (*Santana*) died at age 89

2014 Nina Cassian, Romanian poet and critic died at age 89

2015 At least 10 were killed when the terrorist group Al-Shabab launched an attack on a government building in Somalia

2015 Private company *Space X* launched an unmanned craft filled with supplies to the International Space Station from Cape Canaveral, Florida.

2015 Klaus Bednarz, German journalist and author died at age 72

2015 Percy Sledge, American singer, died at age 74

2015 Archeologists announced they had found at Lomekwi in Kenya 3.3 million-year old stone tools, the oldest ever discovered and which pre-date the earliest known humans

2015 Mark Reeds, Canadian-American ice hockey player and coach died at age 54

2016 A 6.2 earthquake struck Kumamoto, Japan killing at least 6

Curtis Vanaudestrade was born on the same day as Newt Gingrich and Barry Manilow (June 17, 1946) and the infamous Watergate break-in occurred on his birthday. He spent his childhood traveling around the United States and Europe due to his father's career as an executive for the Kaiser Corporation, including his last 2 years of high school in Switzerland where he learned to ski and rock climb as part of the physical education curriculum.

>After a long and varied career, he is now semi-retired in Largo, Florida where he lives with his wife and spends time volunteering for Veterans' programs and organizations working towards sanity in the mental health industry in addition to scouring the news each day for interesting events to add to this series of booklets.

Made in the USA
Columbia, SC
03 April 2022